DEAR FOREVER- LOVE, ME

DEAR FOREVER-LOVE, ME

NIKKI MERRIMAN AND JORDAN FALLERT

CPR Publishing

Copyright © 2024 by Nikki Merriman

All rights reserved. No part of this book may be reproduced in any manner whatsoever without written permission except in the case of brief quotations embodied in critical articles and reviews.

First Printing, 2024

Dedication

To my small army of nieces and nephews, thank you for simultaneously making me feel old and still thinking I'm the cool aunt. I'm naming you all co-presidents of my fan club.

To Rose, the world's best worst service dog, and to the person who will spend forever loving us both.

-Nikki

To the little girl who always wanted to be a writer, the one that became a hopeless romantic. This is for the one who loves so hard, and just wants to be loved in return. This is for her.

To my amazing parents for showing me what real love is, and to my little sisters who I hope get everything they want in life. To my best friend Klaire, I love seeing your happiness, you deserve it all. And to my sweet baby boy Brew. I love you so much and I'm so grateful to have you in my life.

To my Ladies Who Can't Brunch. Thank you for dealing with me on a daily basis and for being an integral part of my life; I hope you all find your happily ever afters. I love you ladies to the moon and back.

-Jordan

Preface

What, exactly, is love? While it has numerous dictionary definitions as both a noun and a verb, a wise blonde by the name of Taylor Swift once said that love is "the most maddening, beautiful, magical, horrible, painful, wonderful, joyous thing in the world." How do you write about a force like love? Does love really stick around forever? Are soulmates real? Why do hearts break? How do you take something so great, so powerful, and contain it to just 200 pages? Honestly, we're going to let you in on a secret:

We don't know. We're just poets. We don't have the answers.

However, what we do know is that love is a force to be reckoned with, a force that has the ability to shatter worlds as well as piece them together all in a single blow. Love crosses miles, oceans, and continents. Love spans decades, emerging stronger every year. Love sees another person and says, "I choose you, even when it's impossible. I see you." Love does see you. Love truly is maddening, beautiful, magical, wonderful, and everything else Taylor said.

Thanks for picking up this book. We're happy you're here.
Xoxo,
Nikki and Jordan

2

I am not the face
that will launch a thousand ships,
I am not the face
that will start wars.
I am the face that you will turn to
when the battlefield of life
wears you down.
I am the face that you turn to
when you're underprepared,
for that smile of reassurance.
But I'm nothing else too grand.

I melt into you,
the stars melt into the moon,
you melt into me,
and before I know it,
"good night"
melts into
"good morning"

How impossible
a love like ours
once seemed.

How too good to be true
you still
sometimes feel.

How lucky am I
to wrap my arms
around a constellation?

"Don't be a 'Pick Me' girl,"
they whisper.

But what is a Pick Me girl?

The type of girl who takes her laptop to the airport
to look mysterious while waiting for her plane.
The girl who goes to dinner by herself,
to take pretty pictures in the rain,
To eat crème brulée,
and just breathe for a while.
And she does that
to escape the pain

But wait,
That's me.

So what if I'm a Pick Me girl?
You say that like it's a bad thing.
Trust me,
It's okay.
I've learned to always pick myself first.

How wonderful it will be
the day we will call our love
an antique:
strong,
aged like fine wine,
and more beautiful than when it first began.

They say if you wait for the
right time,
you'll be waiting forever.
So I jumped;
it's your turn now.

-I promise I'll catch you

I want you
Because you're perfectly imperfect
Like I am, too

And when the end is near
and Father Time says that ours is up,
I'll grasp your hands in mine,
look him in the eye,
and beg him for just a few more seconds
to hold you close

Take my hand
and love me forever

-I dare you

What can I do
to amuse you?

To make your heart race,
pitter patter all over the place?

My whole life I looked for
a place to belong,
somewhere to put down roots,
turn my face to the sun,
and grow.

And then I met you,
and surprisingly to me,
I found myself planting a seed
in your heart;
turns out that place I was looking for
wasn't a place at all.

One day,
I will take your hands in mine,
and promise to love you
forever.

But for now,
I can simply promise you
the stars.

Little did you know that
under the streetlights
cardinals appear,
always watching,
standing still

Time keeps moving;
it stops for no one.

So instead of standing here stuck,
let's move along with it.

Let's run side by side with time,
running,
leaping,
and loving endlessly.

And when we arrive at the end of time,
laughing,
and more in love than ever,
let's look at each other,
out of breath,
and say,
"let's go again."

Picture us,
thirties.
Keys jingling,
new house.
Finally opening that bottle of wine.
White dress,
walking down the aisle,
never say never.

Picture us,
forties.
An old golden retriever
playing fetch in our yard.
Navigating parenthood.
Airplanes,
adventures,
never say never.

Picture us,
eighties.
Grandchildren running
through that same yard.
The squeak of our rocking chairs
telling a lifelong story.
Holding hands,
laughter,
never say never.

Picture us,
together.

We'll keep
growing wild
together,
until eventually
the ink on my skin fades
and our hair turns gray,
and then,
when we turn one hundred,
we'll consider admitting
that we've grown old

One day,
time will come for my long, black hair;
it will surely turn gray.

Time will also come for your gleaming eyes;
they will surely wrinkle.

Just promise me,
when that day comes,
that we won't let time take our souls.

See me.
For who I am—
Not who you want me to be—
because I'm pretty amazing, too.

When all is said and done,
what if this is something
bigger than us both?

Does that scare you
like it scares me?

You pulled me for a kiss
that cold December night,
and all of a sudden we were
a flame
burning in the darkest winter night

You want me to be normal—
I'm not normal,
and I don't want to be.

Find someone else that wants to be trapped.
I just want to be free.

It brings me
the slightest bit of comfort
to know that
however far you end up from me,
our night skies will always share
the same shining stars

When I dream,
you're with me
at the end of the universe,
holding me tight,
kissing my forehead,
telling me that you can't wait
to find me in our next lifetime together.

When I dream,
it's always you
at the end.

Hidden away
in my perfume drawer
is a love letter she wrote to me
in the summer of 2020.

What an honor it is
to have been someone's first love.

What an honor it would be
to be your forever love.

I'm different
but you are too.

You know what it's like
to be handled with kid gloves,
coddled and misunderstood
for something that was out of your control.

You understand,
you see me.

Liking you
was a surprise
out of my control.

But even if you don't like me back,
I'm thankful that I met you.

Fast forward.

Rejection hurts—
even more so
for a romantic like me.

But the day
after you hurt me,
I looked back at this page

Tears welled in my eyes
because all the words
I wrote

were still true;
I'm thankful to have met
someone like you

Dawns are more beautiful
when I spend them
kissing you good morning

Hasn't anyone ever told you?
Time is a thief.
We'll never get back this time together,
so enjoy the present
with me
before it's too late
and you realize
that you can't anymore

I am not your here and now;
I am an always,
an eternity that you take with you,
a backbone.

I am not the girl you leave behind;
I am a commitment,
the woman you bring home,
a family.

I am not just this moment;
I am a forever.

I promise
to hold your hand
like it is the only hand
I'll ever hold

For our first date,
you asked me to see Christmas lights.
I was excited.
No man had taken me to see
Christmas lights.

It sounded fun
and unbelievably romantic.

But I didn't really know you yet.

But I said yes.
I was excited.

And then that little voice
in the back of my mind said
"And what if it doesn't work out?
How will you feel
about Christmas lights then?"

It's funny though,
the tickets were sold out.

So we didn't see
the Christmas lights,
but maybe
that was fate.

Because it didn't work out,
and I would have been reminded of you
every time I saw the trees

and heard the songs.

I'm so thankful.
I wasn't so painfully reminded of you
every Christmas.

Picture this:
Christmas Eve.
Fireplace.
Me and you.
Wrapping paper
and Christmas lights
and Santa cookies.
But let's be honest,
your eyes shine brighter
than every single light
on that goddamn tree.
We lock eyes in a fleeting moment
and we know—
we've made it.

I don't know when I'll be married.
I can't picture my dress,
or the cake,
or who will be there.
I don't know when it'll happen,
or where,
or how.
But I do know,
that when I describe
the perfect forever,
you
roll off my tongue.

Do me one small favor—
don't let me go

Please don't let this all
be a waste of hope

So hold tight to my hand.
I promise
a better life
is just around the bend.

You wake up in the middle of the night
and lock your tired eyes on me
and in that moment
there's nowhere else
I'd rather be

Your velvet hands
know just where to touch me
to melt my soul of stone

Tinder
Tinder and Bumble
Tinder and Bumble and Hinge

The notifications
are a constant jump scare

The false potential
but try, we dare

Try and find our person
in a world not made for love

In a world made
for disappointment,
rejection;
in a world that makes you feel hollow
like you don't have anything at all to love

But you do.

You have something
most people don't—
you have you

There are twenty-four hours in a day;
twenty-four hours
for me to love you
twenty-four different ways

I don't need you
to wrangle the moon;
I simply need you
to sit down beside me
when the world gets too loud

The way the moonlight
dances across your skin—
I don't care if morning
never comes

I don't need an escape plan with you,
that's a first
for me

-I just want to stay

Sometimes
I wonder
where you are

Are you looking
for me
like I'm looking
for you?

Sometimes,
I can't help but feel
human.
But then you come along
and make me feel
celestial

You
were the best part
of that frigid,
freezing,
miserable,
magical
December

Dear Forever,

I hate you.
You take too goddamn long.

I'm sitting in silence
wondering how you can go on.

Don't you feel
that loss?
That ache you just can't
seem to shake?
That's something
I can help you face.

You pull me close
and I swear I can't remember
my life before
those gleaming eyes

I fell in love with you
long before I knew your name

Sometimes it hurts.

I see your shadow
in everything I do,
everything I see,
everything I want to be.

But I haven't even met you yet.

Are you ready to meet me?

I'm done waiting.
Come find me.

-ready or not

You kiss me
and I can taste
an eternity
on your lips

So I'll wait right here beside you
quietly, patiently,
with an outstretched hand,
for more than just a moment
of your vulnerability

Loving you stopped being a choice
when I could no longer tell
where I ended
and you began

Give my love the chance
to change your world

So take my hand,
and let's face this
crazy world
together

I do this all for myself,
to make myself
proud.

With all the strides I've made,
I know I constantly astound.

But in the back of my mind
I'm also doing this for "you."
This imaginary being,
This "you."

Tell me,
have I made "you"
proud yet, too?

I will love you with my hands;
they will take yours
and never let go.

I will love you with my feet;
they will lead the way
when you don't know where to go.

I will love you with my shoulders;
they will carry your load
when life gets too heavy.

I will love you with my eyes;
they will look deeply into yours
and see the vast oceans they hold.

I will love you with my mouth;
it will speak only words
of love, appreciation, affirmation.

I will love you with my heart;
it will beat
only for you.

I will love you
with everything that I am.

I am standing on a beach,
barefoot,
a burning sunset unfolding in the sky.
As the waves crash around me,
I close my eyes,
and all I hear
is your name.

I was not made
for this great unknown.
I know that I was instead made
to love you.

I don't like to write
about things that might be.

I'm afraid I will jinx it.

But I don't know.
Something feels different.
But whatever it is...
I'm excited for the show.

The Chicago snow is falling
(so am I)
Eventually the snow will stop
(I won't)
(but I'm still calling dibs)

I'm not "The One."
I'm not the inferno
that comes quickly and destroys cities.
I'm just a slow ember
that warms hearths and soups.
But that's the thing about embers;
tend to them enough,
and they can become infernos.
So I may not be "The One,"
because you didn't take time
to tend to my fire.

The world is quiet,
and nothing stands between
me
and your touch

-what blessings the night brings

My favorite thing
about our life together
is finding new reasons
to love you more

Stars were born
the night our souls collided;
the sun and the moon
(finally)
held each other
and the universe
would never be the same again

I can't promise life will be easy,
but I can promise
to stand by you despite the mess.
So surrender your heart
to me,
and let's do this
together.

I ask him,
"Be honest,
what do you want?"

He responds quickly
with a single word
that sends my heart racing—
"You."

I will love you even
when we are nothing
but bones
and stardust

And all the things I lost
spilled out in front of me
to form the road
that led to you

I am convinced
that you taste like what
sunshine
must taste like

And I hope life brings you
roses,
and when it does,
I hope you think of me
and smile

May our love shine so bright
it becomes
ingrained
in the cosmos

We could end this now,
cut our losses and leave,
or we could jump
into a love
that could change our lives

-a risk worth taking

In the quiet of the morning,
among the rustling of the trees,
I hear them whispering
"stay"

So dust off your
cracks,
crevices,
and breaks,
and let me fill them in
with love

Do you whisper my name
to the moon
the same way I whisper yours?
In the dead of night,
when midnight has passed,
and even the stars sleep?

-wondering

What's that saying?
Oh yeah.
"If he wanted to, he would."

But don't forget
the second part:
"And if he won't, another man will."

I'm not going to wait on you;
my time is worth too much.

And let's be honest,
you can't afford it.

Let me break it down for you:
life is
infinitely
better
with you in it

And I'm pulling my heart out
through my cracked-open chest,
handing it over to you,
bloody,
but still beating,
and still whole.

Do you see
me now?

You remember
the girl from before—
that innocent,
green-eyed girl
with her nose in a book
and innocence in her eyes.

But now I stand before you
no longer a girl,
but a green-eyed woman,
whose rose colored glasses are
long gone.

So tell me,

do you still want me?

I breathe you in
and you stir my soul.
Galaxies
awaken in parts of me
that I didn't know existed
until they were touched
by your love

When you don't know what to do,
remember—
love is always the answer
(love will outlive us all)

Take my hand;
I've waited
my entire life
for this moment here
with you

We will create
a home for ourselves
where doors don't slam,
bottles don't break,
and eggshells don't cover the floor.
Where footsteps aren't cautious,
walls aren't punched,
and the only secrets kept
are holiday surprises.

We will create
a home for ourselves
that welcomes all,
lights candles,
and celebrates life.
That always has
a warm bed,
a home cooked meal,
and conversations that lift the soul.

We will create
a home for ourselves
that dances,
honors,
and
loves,
loves,
and loves some more.

Books.

That's what I have as models.
Those great love stories.

I aspire
to be the star in an
amazing,
fantastical,
earth-shattering
love story.

The kind that they write
books,
songs,
and sonnets about.

The kind they study in schools,
like a Shakespearean play
without the tragedy,
leaving only the
passionate,
inspiring,
gut-wrenching love story—
a story that deserves
to be shared.

You are the softest light
in the darkest cracks
of my jaded soul

You
are my greatest love letter

I love you
(on purpose)

Our souls slowly became
entangled in one another—
may we never pull them
apart

I want that chemistry
I want that spark
I want that person
who won't leave me after dark

Pull me
closer
closer
closer
until there's not even
an atom between us

Please,
let the world know
we're on our way,
together

Hello.
(be mine)

How are you?
(I want you)

I love you.
(I'd marry you yesterday)

We lock eyes
and I see
a thousand poems unfold
right before my own

-bigger than us

I've always thought
(was conditioned to think)
that love was something
you fought to get,
fought to keep,
fought to earn
(had to earn).

Suffering,
pain,
and love
were synonymous.

After all,
no one is perfect
(right?)

But then.

Enter you.

Enter
(real)
love.

Amid December's cold
you pull me close
(never let go)
you press your lips
to my forehead
(this is it)
and you
don't
let
go
(I'm throwing in the towel)

Three a.m.
isn't the wrong side of midnight
when we're busy
falling more in love

Sometimes
I think too much
about the amount of time
between your texts,
the punctuation that you use.

Did you intend to put
that period there?
Because it made your tone
seem clipped.

Brisk,
tight,
unyielding,
brokering no argument.

I might seem like a
silly girl,
but I'm smart.
I read between lines.
I pick up on tone.

I can sense the most minute changes
in that tone.

With all that being said,
do you still want me?
Because I cannot read you.
I'm starting to feel alone.

I love you
as in, "I see you."

I love you
as in, "I hear you."

I love you
as in, "you're safe here
with me."

I love you
as in,
"stay. "

We danced,
and the world around us
froze;

time stood still
as you spun me around
and around
and around.

Little did I know
your so-called love
would turn out to be
mercurial.

This is me
standing on the mountaintops
of faith,
on the edge
of hope.

This is me,
black hair
and blue eyes
and no parachute,
no contingency plan,
ready to jump.

-catch me

Love does not
stumble,
stagger,
or stall.

Love
lingers,
saunters,
embraces.

Love
adores,
cherishes,
empowers.

Love
affirms,
reveres,
admires.

Love
does not simply
tolerate.

I may not know much,
but I do know
that I am worth
every goddamn chance
that one can take
on love

One day,
when we're old and gray,
and our time on Earth is up,
we'll simply melt into the stars,
becoming one with forever,
immortalized in each other's love

And I'll leave you
with this:

whenever you hear
that Taylor song
we once danced to
in my bedroom
under the midnight moon
as a golden retriever slept,

that song to which
you spun me around
that wooden dance floor
as the band played
and our friends watched,

that song
the piano played
on New Year's Eve
as we danced around that crowded bar,
and you promised me the next fifty years,

I know you'll think of me,
and I hope it haunts you.

You were the first boy.

The first boy I told about this book.

But trust me,
you won't be the last boy
that I'll write about.

I won't give you
that power,
and you won't take
my pen.

Because when the time comes,
you're bound to give in.

DEAR FOREVER- LOVE, ME ~ 111

I have loved you
through every stage of our lives—
your backyard tree
saw the popsicle smiles
on our tiny faces

I have loved you
through every stage of our lives—
those Friday night lights
saw our teenage hands
hold on for dear life

I have loved you
through every stage of our lives—
that Raintree house
saw the end of innocence
but the start of something
so much greater

I have loved you
through every stage of our lives—
that hand-me-down motorcycle
saw us hold each other closer
as we pulled over
to stare at the stars

I have loved you
through every stage of our lives—
that old Civic saw
engagements,
marriages,

kids,
and divorces;
we're still standing

I have loved you
through every stage of our lives—
those phones saw
five hundred ninety-three miles,
two states,
endless hours of up all night,
drop everything and go

I will love you
through every stage of our lives—
an old porch swing
will see us old and wrinkled,
looking back on all this
with smiles and laughter

I have loved you
through every stage of our lives—
it only makes sense
that I will love you through every
stage of the next

And all I need—
all I've ever needed—
is us.

Is me
and you
and forever.

Wherever the universe
has taken you,
I hope life has been good to you
and I hope you know
I think of you
in its quiet
(beautiful)
moments

I wrote this in pen.

Pen,
not pencil.
Because pen means
permanence.
Pencil means
a draft.
It can be erased.

But this?

I don't want this to be
erased.
I want this to last.

I was prepared
to go to war for us—
I readied my words,
grabbed your hand,
and picked up my sword—
but you didn't pick up yours.

Your
"I love yous"
and
"forevers"
disintegrated around us,
and now I wonder—

What is a one-sided war,
anyway?

I hope you know,
in the darkest midnights,
I grieve for the life together
we were looking forward to
(I grieve for what could've been)
(But I'm still looking *forward*)

One day,
you'll lock your eyes on me
and I'll know—
falling in love with you
was always
simply
inevitable

Sure,
we could go through this world
on our own—
growing,
learning,
flourishing—
but just think
how much more
magnificent
it would be
to go through it
t o g e t h e r

I want to be in love—

so in love that I daydream
about a proposal,
a big white wedding,
that earth-shattering,
romantic kiss,
that first dance.

I've never let myself
daydream like that before.

But you make me want to.

Tell me,
how do you go back
to a black-and-white world
after living life in color?

-I'm a rainbow

Take me
at my best;
I will turn you
into a poem
that lifts you
through the clouds
to the heavens.

Leave me
at my worst;
I will turn you
into a poem
that drags you across
the scathing coals.

This is the risk you take
loving
a poet.

Maybe I don't need
a legacy;
maybe these poems
I've written us into
will do the job

You
are every good memory
I have yet to make

I'll turn around
so you can run—
run away from my cares
and my slowly breaking
heart

Maybe in some other life,
the "best friends" trope holds true.

Maybe in some other life,
it's me and you against the world.

Maybe in some other life,
I would've said yes.

-"Champagne Problems," Taylor Swift

Choose me
at noon on a Tuesday
or don't choose me
at all

I'll write about you
until the end of time;
after all,
I'm a poet because of you

-muse

I lose myself
in the hope
that maybe,
at the other end of it all,
it would've been you.

My life is a story:
fantastical
and magical.
I assumed my
love story
would be the same.

I thought maybe
you
would be a main character.

But I guess they're not the same.

The snow fell—
quietly,
beautifully,
gracefully—
and so did I

I didn't know what to do
with the
love
you left behind
when you walked out,
so I turned it into
poetry
that I can only hope
you'll read someday

I know now
that the words I never said
(held back in fear)
were the words you needed to hear
(would've changed everything)

What do I do
with a regret like that?

DEAR FOREVER- LOVE, ME - 135

Never forget that
you
are the
main character
in your story.

Each new chapter
is a new beginning.

You held me close
in that one-bedroom apartment,
and I could've danced with you
for the rest of eternity
(if only you'd have let me)

I will love you—
fiercely,
wildly,
intensely
love you—
through this lifetime.

Just like I did
in the last.

And just like I will
in the next.

They say to write what you know,
but there are only
so many ways
to spell out your name

I hear that song,
and I close my eyes,
and I'm whisked right back
to that midnight bedroom
and you are
dancing away with my heart

-"I Don't Dance," Lee Brice

So I'll write you into
yet another poem,
another page,
another book,
because when I do,
for a moment—
just a moment—
you're here with me

My forever
won't make me feel
like I'm too much.

My forever
won't make me feel
like I'm not enough.

They will be grateful for my time;
they will love my long stories
that go off the rails.

They will join in my laughter
and revel in my wins.

They will kiss me sweetly
and tell me softly

that I'm all they need to win.

I laid my head on your shoulder
and everyone else
melted away,
and the laughter faded,
and nothing mattered
but the two of us

-our last night

I never did love the cold,
but then it brought me you

"We never even dated,"
I tell myself as I
sigh,
sit down in my chair,
and slowly start
to cry.

You should have been my first.
My first hand-hold,
my first kiss,
my first lover.

You need to be my last.

Maybe the universe just knew
it would be you all along

You
are my heart's
most beautiful beginning

Not even an ocean
could keep our hearts apart

This long road
is worth every mile
as long as
you
are at the end of it

Forever,
forever,
forever—

why do you take
so damn long?

I will find you.
Lifetime after lifetime,
I will find you.

Somewhere within
this hazy world,
our souls found each other

You waltzed into my heart
as if the universe were saying,
"here is the love
I promised you."

You wrap me up in you
and suddenly it hits me—
this is what home feels like

I'm thankful that
my heart is a vital organ.

Because if I didn't need it,
I would give it away
for free
to someone who didn't deserve it;
then where would I be?

This
here
with you
has been my favorite surprise

Love me
safely,
love me
wildly,
love me
freely—
love me in the way
that only you can

The only one for you
is me,
and the only one for me
is the stars.
But don't you know
you hold the universe
in your palm?

Your heart
is my safest haven

Some things
are better left unsaid.

But sometimes,
I can't help it.

Out tumble the words
that my heart needs you to hear;
please don't let them go unheard,

I beg of you.

Yours is the hand I'll reach for
at every golden sunrise

I have a feeling
that this could shine
brighter
than any star

Let me rest
here in your arms
(at home)
just a little while longer

-it's not goodbye, it's see you later

I never thought
you
would be the one
I write about,
but here I am,
the words flowing from my pen
as my heart sings your name

I cannot wait to do
great things
with you

Here's the thing about this book of poetry—

It may be called
"Dear Forever- Love, Me,"

but it should be renamed.

Because at this point,
it should be called

"Dear Forever-
you took your sweet fucking time, didn't you?"

Press your body
to mine,
your palms
against my back,
and never let me go

Let's start
our forever
right now

Call me
crazy,
but maybe,
just maybe,
I could spend
all of my forevers
with you

If my tears
could form an ocean,
my god,
I'd trade my life
for yours
and then drown in them

I may not know much,
but I do know
that I love you
so much more
than I did
yesterday

The many curveballs of life
make me feel like a
baseball player;
but where are all of my
adoring fans?

I'm ready to step up to the plate;
let's knock this love story
out of the park.

My favorite part of
me
has always been
you

-don't go

The tears already
flow freely
from the depths of my soul;
this is just
a rough sketch
of what losing you
looks like

Remember:
when all is said
and done,
the love between us
will outlive all this

-a poem for a rainy day

Someday,
from the moon
we'll watch the Earth,
watching the little ones
grow old,
watching the legacies
you built
in your
(too short)
time there

-I'll grow old in memory of you

How do you prepare yourself
for the death
of everything
that lights your way?
For the death
of a star so bright,
even the moon
will be outshone?

One day,
all too soon,
I will wake up a different person
(you didn't wake up at all)
(I still promise to hold your hand)

I just want
(need)
more
and more
and more
of you
(I'll never get enough)

I find myself
longing for spring,
but I so easily forget that
I spent the harshest of winters
falling in love
with you

This is life.
This is now our
(ugly)
(dreadful)
(shocking)
life.
Whether I'm ready
or unprepared,
strong enough
or still too weak,
I'm doing it with you.

-hold on tight

You
were the last thing
my heart saw coming,
but you were exactly what
my soul needed

I'm ready
for that forever love,

to put a smile
on someone's face
everyday,

to be the reason
they look at the sidewalk
and smile.

They say
(I really wouldn't know)

that when you love someone
you start to crave.
You crave their scent,
their perfume,
their cologne,
their musk,
their pheromones;

I'm ready to crave.

Let me put it
as simply as I can:
when you die,
I will too.
(I won't know how to survive)

Through this
whirlpool of uncertainty,
I promise one thing
for certain:
I will love you
even harder

Forgive my silence;
some things
even leave the poet
at a loss for words

They say
if a writer loves you,
then you'll never die.
So I'll write you into
page,
after page,
after page,
folding a thousand paper hearts,
hoping you'll never desert us.
But
HOPE
is a four-letter word.

I breathe you in
(inhale)
and out comes poetry
(exhale)

You
are my kind
of love
(the forever kind)

Only the moon
knows
that I spend my nights
begging it
for your life

I will love you
until the end of time
(just tell me how)

The fact that a poet like me
still dares to dream
(of a love like ours)
is nothing short of a
miracle

I wonder what it's like
to be so
in love.

I've only seen it
in movies
or
in books.

At this point,
I think it's a myth—
something used to
keep us
on the hook.

You
are the best part
of this
crazy
little
life

We're surrounded
by so many great
love stories,
but
ours
is easily my
favorite

-I can't wait to tell it

Growing up,
I wanted to be an author.
But sitting down
to write a story
overwhelmed me.

But then
I became a poet.

My name is on a book
forever.

It is unbelievable—
my name going down
in history
for bringing joy,
maybe a smile,
or a distraction,
to people's lives.

So thank you,
life,
for making me a poet.

But why do I even
dare to hope?
Hope always makes
a complete fool out of me.

I guess that's why the term is
"hopeless romantic."

I wanted you to be
a safe place;
You seemed like you were at the start.
But I slowly started to understand
that you were just
playing games
with my heart.

I asked you nicely
not to,
but I guess you were a liar
all along.

Maybe you should talk about that
with your therapist
next Tuesday,
before my heart breaks
further apart.

Airports.

They bring me back
into your arms,

but then
they take me away.

-love/hate relationships

We found each other
one February night
under that king-sized blanket—
cold feet,
warm hearts,
and the promise
of so much love ahead

I want a love like my parents';
they are so
patient
with each other,
so kind.
Their eyes light up
when they speak
to each other.

I want a love like that—
one to call
mine.

This love has not simply been
a love for the ages;
this love has been a love for the
universe,
for the eons,
and for every single lifetime,
past,
present,
and future.

About The Author

Nikki is a runner, dancer, artist, model, and traumatic brain injury survivor from the Chicagoland area. When she isn't writing, she enjoys painting, skydiving, traveling, baseball, and spending time with her family and pets. More often than not, you can find her on the beach or near the water. There are few things she enjoys more than hearing from her readers; you can find her and more of her work on Instagram @nixwrites_.

About The Author

As a traumatic brain injury survivor, Jordan has learned the importance of living life to the fullest. She loves fitness, traveling, reading, and is obsessed with the color green. When she isn't working out or writing, she is usually with her family, her dog, or outside in the sun.